BOOK ONE

Roots of racism

INSTITUTE OF RACE RELATIONS
2-6 Leeke Street, King's Cross Road, London WC1X 9HS, UK

Seventh impression, 1996

© Institute of Race Relations 1982
  ISBN 0 85001 023 3
Published and distributed by the Institute of Race Relations.
Designed by Hilary Arnott and Susan Hobbs.
Maps by Sandra Oakins.
Typeset by Range Left (TU), 01-251 3959.
Printed by the Russell Press (TU), Radford Mill, Norton Street, Nottingham NG7 3HJ.
Cover photo from *Princely India: photos by Raja Deen Dayal, 1884-1890*,
edited by C. Worswick, Hamish Hamilton, 1980.

Contents

Introduction		iv
Chapter one	'If you're white . . .'	1
Chapter two	Europe's early history	4
Chapter three	The dominance of Spain and Portugal	8
Chapter four	Colonisation	13
Chapter five	The colonial system and the Industrial Revolution	17
Chapter six	Slavery and racism	21
Glossary		28

Introduction

In our evidence to the Rampton Committee of Inquiry into the Education of Children from Ethnic Minority Groups, we argued that the development and promotion of multi-cultural studies did nothing to tackle the fundamental issue of racism.

While multi-cultural studies, in explaining differences in customs and culture, may help modify attitudes, such studies are primarily an extension of existing educational techniques and methods, and, as such, allow racism within society, and within the educational system itself, to pass unchallenged. Thus our evidence stated, 'education itself comes to be seen in terms of an adjustment process within a racialist society and not as a force for changing the values that make that society racialist'. 'Ethnic minorities do not suffer disabilities because of ethnic differences as such . . . but because such differences are given differential weightage in a system of racial hierarchy.'

Therefore, our concern 'is not centrally with multi-cultural, multi-ethnic education but with anti-racist education (which by its very nature would include the study of other cultures). Just to learn about other people's cultures, though, is not to learn about the racism of one's own. To learn about the racism of one's own culture, on the other hand, is to approach other cultures objectively.'

Such an approach demands the questioning and re-examination of basic assumptions and accepted values on the part of both teachers and students. Through our work over many years, with teachers, students, children and librarians, we have become increasingly aware of the dearth of any material for young people which provides the basis for such a re-evaluation.

These two books, *Roots of racism* and *Patterns of racism*, are an attempt to begin meeting that need. They cover, in a way which is unique in either the school curriculum or in literature for young people, the history of black-white relations from the vantage point of the black experience. They attempt to reach to the core of racist beliefs, to show, for example, that civilisations rise and fall and none is 'superior' for all time, that the concept of European 'discovery' is a myth, as is that of European pre-eminence in ability, inventiveness or level of achievement. In doing so, they demonstrate the undeniable link between the growth and development of racism and the processes of the economic system.

In thus dealing seriously with an alternative view of the nature and development of British society, these materials we hope will help pupils – both black and white – to develop a critical judgement, not only of their beliefs and values but of contemporary social institutions, prevailing attitudes, orthodoxies past and present, and their interrelationship with the actual structure of society.

Because this project is part of our ongoing work, we would welcome responses and feed back to it, and will be happy to give teachers who wish to use it what further help we can. Our own limited resources would never have stretched to such a publishing project and we wish, therefore, to record our sincere thanks to the Calouste Gulbenkian Foundation for their vision in funding it, and their patience in seeing it through. Without their assistance, it could not have become a reality.

A. Sivanandan
Director
Institute of Race Relations

CHAPTER ONE

'If you're white...'

If you're white
You're all right
If you're brown
Stick around
If you're black
Get back

That's from a black American folk song. We can recognise straightaway what it describes so simply – an arrangement of society, where each person's level or position is defined by the colour of his or her skin. It is a relationship of inequality, based on skin colour, with the whites on top and the blacks below.

We are familiar with it as 'race relations' or the 'race problem'. We know that, in broad terms, it applies not just to the USA, but to nearly all the countries of the world in which both white and non-white people live. And, if we look at the world as a whole, we can see that the same relationship of inequality persists, between the white and non-white nations of the world. It is the white nations which have, and appear determined to keep at any cost, wealth, and therefore power, grossly out of proportion to the size of their populations, and it is the non-white nations which struggle relentlessly for justice and equality.

But there is in fact no such thing as different races, not scientifically speaking. Despite all the years of investigating and charting – this blood group and that, this bone structure and that, this disease and that – scientists have found no biological characteristics that belong exclusively to any one group of the world's

'The whites on top and the blacks below.' This picture shows officers (always white men) and lascars (black seamen) on HIMS Hardinge during Lord Curzon's tour of the Persian Gulf, 1903. Black crews were taken on, whenever required, from all over Britain's Empire. They were paid much less than white crews.

COURTESY HAMISH HAMILTON

people. Separate 'races' do not exist. All we are left with are the scientifically meaningless variations of skin colour.

Yet there is racial inequality – inequality of treatment as between black and white people. So we see that distinctions based on 'race' (i.e. skin colour) can only be understood as social distinctions. The details of how these distinctions are worked out and put into practice may vary widely from one society to another, and may vary from one historical period to another. But always at their root is the attempt to keep a particular group of people, marked out by the colour of their skin, in the lowest section of society, to keep them poor and powerless.

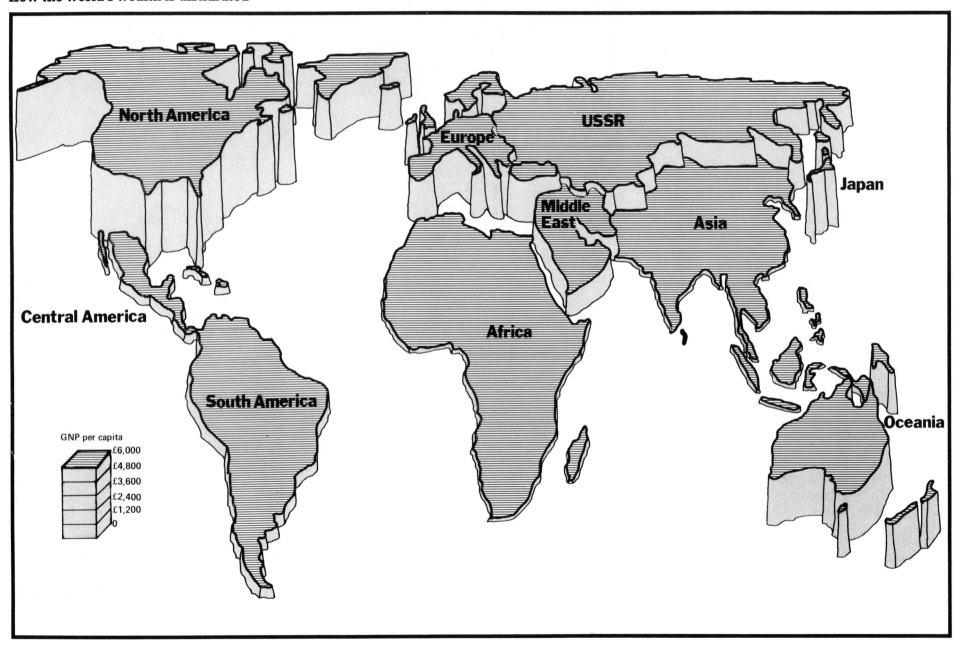

North America

Europe

USSR

Japan

Middle East

Asia

Central America

Africa

South America

Oceania

GNP per capita
£6,000
£4,800
£3,600
£2,400
£1,200
0

It is the continuing resistance to this fundamental injustice that has led, in our own time, to racial violence in the cities of Europe and North America, and to racial wars in Africa. It is significant that those countries which have made the greatest commitment to developing societies which are not arranged on the basis of skin colour are some of the newly independent countries of Africa which for centuries had been on the receiving end of racial injustice – countries like Tanzania, Zimbabwe, Mozambique and Guinea-Bissau.

If we are to make sense of 'race relations' in our modern world, how the 'race problem' has developed, and what lies behind it, we must first go back through history in order to look at the 400 years previous to this century, when Europe dominated the rest of the world, most of it non-white.

Further reading

N. File and Chris Power, *Black Settlers in Britain 1555-1958* (London, Heinemann, 1981).

International Defence and Aid Fund, *Children under apartheid* (London, IDAF, 1980).

M. Kidron and Ronald Segal, *State of the World Atlas* (London, Pluto/Heinemann, 1981).

Joyce Sikakane, *Window on Soweto* (London, Pluto, 1980).

Suggestions for work

Using the Pluto atlas, take three countries and compare them in terms of their populations, their natural resources, and their industries. How does the standard of living compare between these three countries?

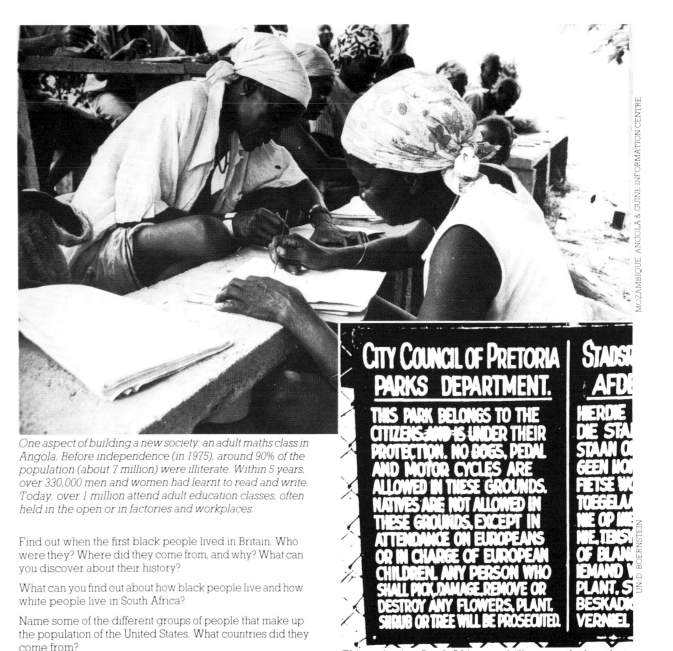

One aspect of building a new society: an adult maths class in Angola. Before independence (in 1975), around 90% of the population (about 7 million) were illiterate. Within 5 years, over 330,000 men and women had learnt to read and write. Today, over 1 million attend adult education classes, often held in the open or in factories and workplaces.

Find out when the first black people lived in Britain. Who were they? Where did they come from, and why? What can you discover about their history?

What can you find out about how black people live and how white people live in South Africa?

Name some of the different groups of people that make up the population of the United States. What countries did they come from?

This notice in a South African park illustrates the lengths to which a society based on divisions of race can go.

3

CHAPTER TWO

Europe's early history

Influences and ideas

Do you know who first invented the wheel? Who invented writing? Who discovered the science of astronomy? Who developed the science of mathematics? The ancient civilisations of the world which grew up around river basins (for example, Sumer, India, Egypt and China) made many important discoveries and inventions which are still basic to our way of life today. Each civilisation benefited to some extent from the ideas and inventions of those which had developed before it. Each had a period in which it flourished and prospered, before it decayed or was overtaken by a new and different civilisation. By the time, therefore, that we see the beginnings of a modern, European-wide civilisation developing, it had not only the resources of the ancient civilisations of Greece and Rome to draw upon, but also those of the East and North Africa.

Europe expands

By the end of the 15th century, Europeans had made rapid progress in science and technology. Their builders had learnt to erect huge and lofty cathedrals, using the principle of the arch to hold up great towers and stone roofs – a technique learnt from the domed and arched buildings of the East. The use of unwieldy Roman numbers, which are impossible to add together without using a counting device, was replaced by the **Arabic** numbers we know today –

Compare the interior of the great Mosque of Cordoba (left), built in the 10th century by the Moors in Southern Spain, with the Galilee Chapel in Durham Cathedral (right), built in the 11th and 12th centuries.

making more sophisticated and precise scientific calculation possible. The most advanced medical techniques and understanding that Europe possessed had filtered down indirectly from the great North African civilisation of ancient Egypt. The science of astronomy was being developed (learnt from the techniques of the ancient Greeks and the Egyptians) – of vital importance for **navigation**. Some thinkers already understood that the world was round, from observing the movement of the planets.

Among the ideas which came to Europe from other civilisations were those in the **nautical** sciences, printing and paper making and explosives. It was these ideas which, when developed and put into use, enabled Europeans to explore and expand beyond their known world, to sail and chart the seas, to publish their knowledge of them, and to conquer and rule the peoples whom they found beyond them.

Trade and enrichment

But why did they do these things? What were the driving forces? To understand this, we must understand some of the pressures within Europe itself, in its early history. Throughout the 11th, 12th and 13th centuries, Europe's population grew and peasants and farmers cleared wastelands and swamps to grow more food. The frontiers of Christian Europe itself were pushed out – in the east, Germans and Scandinavian peoples conquered and converted the Baltic and Slavic peoples; Cyprus, Crete and, for a short time, Palestine and Syria were conquered in the Crusades, and some of the wealth brought back to Europe; Spain was reconquered from the Moors, a Muslim people. In Britain, there was English **expansion** into Wales, Scotland and Ireland.

Trade grew up – carried on by men who, for one reason or another, were no longer tied to the land, as the vast majority of European peasants were. These men travelled from place to place, exchanging the small **surplus** of produce from one area for other goods elsewhere. Some of that trade was long distance – though Palestine and Syria did not stay under Christian rule for long, trade between them and the great Italian cities continued.

As the population grew, the market for agricultural produce grew, and so did the need to farm more efficiently. In some parts of Europe, early industries were already growing up – the wool industry in

---

Land is cleared and farmed. The population increases. Trade grows up. Peasant farmers have to feed the whole of society.

Lords and nobles and clergy make more and more demands – better foods, heavier taxes to pay for finer luxuries and bigger private armies. Peasant farming can't keep up. Peasants rebel.

Society is in chaos. Millions are dying of plague. The lords have only one answer – fighting and war. War destroys settled farming. Greater poverty, greater hunger, greater desperation.

What next?

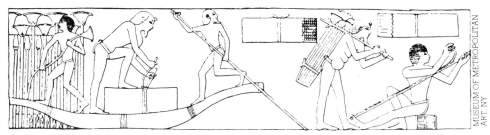

Above: Egyptians collecting and preparing papyrus plant to make paper, around 1500 BC.
Right: How German monks in the 13th century stretched (centre picture), smoothed (right-hand picture) and finally cut (left-hand picture) parchment for their manuscripts.

Flanders, for example. By the end of the 12th century, England was exporting corn to Flanders, and by the 13th century, English lords were beginning to find it **profitable** to turn over the lands on which the peasants grew their crops to sheep farming, so as to sell wool to Flemish merchants (though this development did not really gather speed till later).

Crisis

Then, throughout the 14th and the first half of the 15th century, Europe underwent a massive and severe

> ❝ Forsooth . . . your sheep that were wont to be so meek and tame and so small eaters now . . . become so great devourers and wild, that they eat up and swallow down the very men themselves . . . Noblemen and gentlemen . . . enclose all into pastures . . . and leave nothing standing. The husbandmen be thrust out of their own . . . by hook or crook they must needs depart away, poor silly wretched souls, men, women, husbands, wives, fatherless children, widows, woeful mothers with their young babies . . . finding no place to rest in. ❞
>
> *Thomas More*

crisis which shook the whole of its society. For centuries this had been ordered in the same basic, unchanging pattern, with peasants working the land not only to produce their own meagre food, but to support the lord and his household, and the Church and its clergy. As we have seen, during this time Europe slowly expanded its agriculture, its population and its trade. Then, suddenly, this steady growth gave way to a sharp decline.

There is no single simple explanation for this. It may be that the land had become exhausted and, although improvements in farming had been made, it simply could not produce enough to feed the growing population. The climate also changed, winters becoming longer and more severe and the growing season shorter. In particular, the burden on the peasant increased as he and she had to support greater numbers of lords and nobles and their families. At the same time, the wealthy were demanding more meat in their diet – and so land that the peasant farmer had used for growing his food was instead used for cattle. Increasing burdens of taxation were also forced on to the peasant, to pay for his lord's household and followers, as well as to satisfy the lord's growing appetite for luxuries and fine and costly goods. But the peasantry did not accept its lot passively; in England, France and Germany there were fierce and bitter revolts from around the middle of the 14th century onwards. And when the peasants

of England marched on London (in 1381), they came close to overthrowing the King and his government.

Famine, war and the search for an alternative

From 1348 onwards, the plague swept across Europe year after year, killing millions, and the poor people and the peasants, with their low quality diet, had little resistance to it. The plague was followed by more famine and scarcity – resulting in even more deaths

The spread and extent of the plague

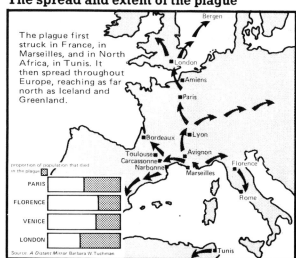

The plague first struck in France, in Marseilles, and in North Africa, in Tunis. It then spread throughout Europe, reaching as far north as Iceland and Greenland.

proportion of population that died in the plague

PARIS		
FLORENCE		
VENICE		
LONDON		

Source *A Distant Mirror* Barbara W Tuchman

The goods come from far away. The stranger is a **MERCHANT!**

He comes from the far-off city of Venice.

PROGRESSIVE LABOR

and greater hardships.

Local warfare and fighting had always been part of European society, but in the period we are discussing this too went beyond all bounds. Europe was ravaged and exhausted by the constant warfare of its lords (the most obvious example is the Hundred Years War, which lasted from 1335 to 1435), as each tried to claw back some security and stability, some prosperity at his neighbour's expense. But they were trying to fight their way out of a state of affairs which fighting only made worse. Such continuous warfare, the further destruction it caused to settled agriculture, and the social chaos that followed made the peoples of Europe more needy than ever, and their rulers violently determined to seize on anything they could turn to their advantage, any opportunity for making wealth.

A new society in the making

The old social order of medieval Europe was cracking under the strain, and the search for a more secure existence propelled men in many different directions. Some, believing more gold to be the solution to their problems, turned to alchemy, and the

An alchemist tries to make gold. From a 16th century German woodcut.

John Ball rides to meet Wat Tyler, a leader of the Peasants' Revolt. His followers, though, appear here much better dressed and fitted out then they would really have been.

search for the magic formula which could turn ordinary metals into gold. Others, through **astrology** and supernatural methods, tried to harness and control the natural world. Others, like the priest John Ball, believed that all land should be held in common, and that the lords and the Church should be driven from their positions of power over the peasants' lives.

The search of others to seize, control and make use of the resources in the world around them led ultimately, by fits and starts, and over hundreds of years, to the type of highly organised commercial and industrial society we live in today. It led, in short, to our modern world.

Further Reading

B. Catchpole, *The clash of cultures* (London, Heinemann, 1980), Chapter 3, 'Crusades in the Holy Land'
L. Cowie, *The Black Death and the peasants' revolt* (London, Wayland, 1972).
Leo Huberman, *Man's worldly goods: the story of the wealth of nations,* Part 1 (New York and London, Monthly Review, 1968)
M. Price, *The peasants' revolt* (Harlow, Longman, 1980).

Suggestions for work

Discuss as a group what you think you learn from other societies and cultures. What previous inventions and innovations can you discover that Europeans learnt from other civilisations?

What was the life of the peasants in Europe in the Middle Ages like? What food did they grow? What did they live on? What services did they have to do for the Lord of the Manor?

Find out about the events of the Peasants' Revolt. Why did the peasants take such a desperate step? What were they fighting for? Why were the King and the government so eager to defeat them?

What were the Crusades? What were their results? What benefits did they bring to Europe? How did the Muslim peoples fight back?

CHAPTER THREE

The dominance of Spain and Portugal

Land and gold were sought above all. It was the need for them, as the situation within Europe became more and more desperate, that drove Europeans out beyond Europe's own frontiers.

Of course, there were other motives as well. Simple curiosity – the human urge to widen the horizons of knowledge – must have played a part. (A journey beyond known seas was then, perhaps, even more of a 'journey into the unknown' than is a journey into space today.) Moreover, just as the 14th century had been one of enormous turmoil and conflict in society as a whole, so this turmoil and conflict also showed itself in the realm of ideas and beliefs.

The Church and society

Let us think about this for a minute. It is very difficult for us today to imagine how powerfully the Christian

Church dominated people's thinking, attitudes and beliefs, and how important it was in attempting to regulate society. All the life of society was organised around it, including education and the care of the sick and the poor. It concerned itself with, and attempted to direct, every human activity – what you ate, how you dressed, how you behaved. Christian teaching provided the groundwork of ideas and theories from which men set out to understand and explain the world around them. But this teaching could itself be opened up to many different interpretations, could be developed in different ways as people sought to grapple with the concrete problems and difficulties of their societies.

Just as the social order had been shaken from top to bottom, and put under colossal strains, so hitherto accepted beliefs came to be questioned and argued

These pictures from Avicenna's 'Canon of Medicine' show one of the medical techniques (in this case for dislocated joints) that became known to Europe through the work of Muslim scholars. Avicenna – his true name was Ibn Sena – was a Persian who lived in the 11th century. Through his work, much scientific and medical knowledge was transmitted to Europe.

over, leading to new ideas, new ways of looking at and understanding the world. The advances made in scientific understanding, the knowledge and learning gleaned from great libraries in the East, raised as many questions as they answered. And this new learning had somehow to be dealt with in the framework of Christian teaching. Such an opening up of the 'frontiers of the mind' must also have stimulated the urge to explore and discover.

Glory . . .

Then, too, there was glory, not so much for the explorers themselves, nor even just their Kings and Queens and countries, but for God. Spain and Portugal, both early colonising powers, had themselves been conquered and ruled by the Moors, a Muslim people from North Africa. In their struggles to drive out the Moors, and in their Crusades, or holy wars, against the Muslim religion, the Spanish and Portuguese had developed an aggressive and warlike Christianity which saw Islam as its deadly enemy, whose followers should be converted by the sword.

Although the Moors had been finally driven out, the warlike nature of Spanish and Portuguese Christian belief still remained, and led this time to the conquest of new lands and the forced conversion of their peoples to the Kingdom of God. (In Christian thinking, no one could be fully human till they had been brought into the one, true Church.) Thus they could combine their Christian duty with what also brought them practical advantage.

. . . and gold

For, when all is said and done, the greatest driving force must have come from the need to increase wealth, trade and the production of food. Throughout the Middle Ages, trade had not only been carried on within Europe (in grains, wool, salt and meat and,

The main European trade routes in the 15th century

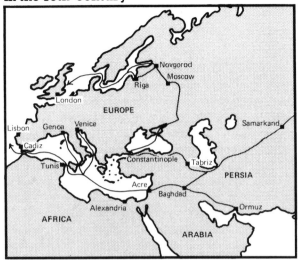

around the Mediterranean, in slaves), but with the East (with countries, that is, such as India and China), in goods which had become invaluable to Europe's rulers, such as spices, silks and precious stones. These goods were paid for with Europe's silver and the gold it had traded from North Africa. The trade route, however, often entirely overland, via many middlemen (including Arab merchants), was long, dangerous and expensive. A sea route between Europe and the East would, therefore, be a great advantage.

It was the search for this sea route which led the Portuguese, from the middle of the 15th century, to edge their way down the west coast of Africa, trading on their way for gold, ivory and African slaves. They had already **colonised** the islands in the Atlantic – Madeira and the Azores – and were using them to grow grains, sugar, dyes and wine, and, if you look at the map, you will see how well placed Portugal was to take this next step. Both the currents and winds were favourable. By 1487, the Portuguese reached the Cape of Good Hope and by 1499, Vasco da Gama had sailed round the tip of Africa, up its east coast, across

the Indian ocean and back home to Portugal. India and the rest of Asia were now open to trade and **exploitation** by Europe.

Meanwhile, the Spanish, in search of the same goal, had been 'discovering' the rest of the world. (Discovering it for Europeans, that is; those who lived there, of course, already knew it existed.) In 1492, Christopher Columbus, trying to find India by sailing west instead of east, 'bumped' into the Caribbean islands (which Europeans did not know were there). The islands thus became known as the 'West Indies'.

Soon, other Spanish explorers found south and central America – and with them their gold and silver. These precious metals were becoming increasingly

Portuguese penetration of Africa

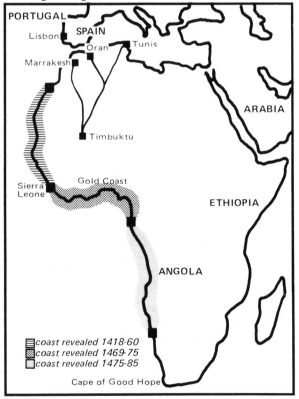

coast revealed 1418-60
coast revealed 1469-75
coast revealed 1475-85

Cape of Good Hope

> **"** Of gold is treasure made, and with it he who has it does as he wills in the world and it even sends souls to Paradise. **"**
>
> *Columbus*

important, for they represented wealth in themselves, and were the means by which international trade could be carried on. More and more gold and silver was needed for coinage. Europe's own silver mines produced very little by comparison. The Spanish conquest and expansion which followed was characterised not by trade, but by plunder. That is to say, the Spanish **conquistadores** robbed and murdered – not individual people – but peoples, on a massive scale.

The Aztecs and the Incas

Cortes, whom many of us were taught to consider a hero, was in fact the man who plundered and destroyed the highly developed Aztec society of Mexico, and stole the gold of its temples for Spain. Pisarro, in much the same manner as Cortes, destroyed the Inca civilisation in Peru and robbed that country of its wealth. In doing so, the Spaniards claimed that the Aztecs and the Incas were barbarous savages, who needed to be civilised. No doubt the stories helped justify the conquistadores' own savagery – but the truth is that these were huge well-organised empires in which lived millions of people. The diversity of their agriculture and their skill in maintaining the fertility of their land were far in advance of what Europe was capable of at that time. Europe later took from them the cultivation of such crops as maize, tobacco, potatoes and even tomatoes.

At the time of the Spanish conquest, the empire of the Incas was already being torn apart in a civil war, so it was vulnerable to the guns and cannons of the foreign invaders. For the one decisive advantage which Europe possessed in this period, and which was to count for more than all the developments in science, art and social organisation among the societies it was to conquer, was the development of firearms. One result of Europe's long years of internal warfare had been the development – when everything else was going downhill – of more efficient and powerful weapons. Guns can kill instantaneously, from a distance and, unless the other side has similar equipment, in comparative safety. Such a means of destruction would strike terror into those it was directed against.

Yet even this would not have ensured the Spanish conquest and control of these huge regions had it not been for the diseases that the conquistadores brought with them. It was the fevers, the smallpox, the measles, the chicken pox, diseases against which the Indians (as the native American peoples were called) had no resistance, that killed them off in huge numbers and enabled the Spaniards to conquer them. In the same way, by disease as much as by the sword, the Spaniards wiped out the Carib and Arawak peoples of the West Indies and took over their land. (Indeed, by the 17th century, European colonisers had begun to use germ warfare deliberately against native Americans as a cheap and quick means of ridding territories of their inhabitants.)

Exploitation

Soon, of course, there was little left to plunder, except the land itself – and that the Spanish and Portuguese could not take with them, so they began to settle on it. They mined for silver, using at first the labour of the

> 66 Aztecs, Incas and Mayas totalled between 70 and 90 million when the foreign conquerors appeared on the horizon; a century and a half later they had been reduced to 3.5 million. 99
>
> *Galeano*

native Americans, whom they enslaved, and attempted to raise cattle and grow crops. But so harsh were their conditions, and so fierce their resistance that the Indians died in thousands and the population of the Americas, or the New World as it also came to be known, dropped drastically. So the colonists turned to the nearest accessible source of labour for the mines and plantations – Africa – from which they took slaves in great numbers (some slave trading on a small scale was already being carried on from there by Arab merchants).

The very term 'Latin America' as a name for this region of the world shows how deep and lasting has been the effect on it of Portuguese and Spanish colonialism. The mixture of peoples who make up the populations of Latin America still shows up the social order the colonists first imposed, with the native American peoples at the very poorest and most deprived end of society.

The scramble for riches

But the Spanish and Portuguese were soon to be overtaken by other European powers. During the 17th century, they faced increasing competition as colonisers and for control of trade, especially the slave trade, from other up and coming European powers. These were firstly Holland, then France and Britain – countries which in an earlier period had been kept out of the profitable trade in and around the Mediterranean, which was controlled by the wealthy Italian cities.

A view of the Inca city of Cuzco in Peru shortly after the conquest. The biggest building you can see is the temple.

These countries were, in their turn, rapidly developing and reorganising their agriculture, trade and commerce. They had learnt from and improved on the nautical and ship-building skills of the Spanish and Portuguese and were acquiring new skills and new technologies. Spain, on the other hand, was beset with internal difficulties, rebellion, warfare and long-standing rivalry with France, which weakened its control over overseas trade.

The decline of Spain was marked in 1588 by the destruction of its fleet – the famous Armada – by Britain, with the help of a storm. (Portugal, in an effort

The ruins of the temple at Chichén-Itzà, a Mayan city. The Mayas were one of the ancient civilisations of South America (they came before the Aztecs and the Incas) who, among other things, developed the sciences of astronomy and mathematics to a high degree.

Caribs in St Lucia attacking the crew of a British ship, the St John, *in 1608.*

to stave off its own decline, had reunited with Spain some eight years earlier.) After this, Holland, France and Britain began to compete with each other for the worldwide trade and territories of Portugal and Spain in which the slave trade played a vital and increasingly important part. For the growing merchant classes of these countries, this was no more than the logical extension of their activities in Europe – remember the trade that had been carried on in Europe in the Middle Ages.

With the discovery and conquest of new lands, the amount of this trade increased enormously, and

Gold mining under the Spanish. From Theodore de Bry, Historia Americae, 1590-1634.

BRITISH MUSEUM

* E. Galeano, *Open veins of Latin America* (New York and London, Monthly Review Press, 1972).
Lennox Honychurch, *The Caribbean people*, Book 1 (London, Nelson Caribbean, 1979), Chapters 3 and 4.

Suggestions for further work

What can you find out from the books listed above about the ancient civilisations of the Aztecs and the Incas? How big were they? How did their people live? How did the European conquest affect them?

What can you find out about the trade that was carried on in the Mediterranean (including the trade in slaves) and controlled by great Italian cities, like Venice and Genoa?

How long did Spain and Portugal rule over the various countries of Latin America? How did the native Americans and the Africans brought in as slaves attempt to fight back? (The second book in this series will help you here.)

Discuss why you think the merchants of Europe were eager to take part in colonial ventures.

further enriched the merchants. They set up companies – one of the first was called the Merchant Adventurers – that took much of the trade with the East away from Portugal. They competed with each other for the African slave trade. And they colonised territories in Africa, Asia and America.

Further reading

(* indicates more difficult texts)

E. Braithwaite and A. Phillips, *The people who came*, Book 3 (Harlow, Longman Caribbean, 1972), especially Chapter 8.
* Philip Foner, *History of Black Americans* (London and New York Greenwood, 1975), Chapters 6 and 7.

CHAPTER FOUR

Colonisation

How it began

Let us look at this period of colonisation in a little more detail, and try to understand what was happening, and why, for it was in this period that the basis was laid for Europe to dominate, by the end of the 19th century, almost the whole world.

The wealth built up and added to in the early eras of plunder and commerce had made the merchants of Europe far richer, and so more economically powerful, than ever. As this group of men grew in size,

Sir Walter Raleigh brings back tobacco to Europe: 'And then you do what with it Walt? . . . You roll it up, you put it in your mouth . . . no you're kidding . . . you set fire to it?' (Apologies to Bob Newhart)

wealth and influence, as they developed their ideas of what it was in their interest to do, and what was not in their interest to do, so we can begin to talk of them as a class in society.

Their prime motive was to make more money, and they were ready to put the money they already had into anything, from slave trading and piracy to the more respectable businesses of commerce, in order to make such a profit. The more they could buy goods at the lowest possible price from one place, and sell them at the highest possible price in another, the more profit they could make. Though they did not themselves sail the slave trading ships, they put up the money, in return for a good share in the profits, that enabled others to do so. Hence we call them merchant **capitalists**.

The Reformation

The Christian Church (which as we have seen concerned itself with every aspect of society) had taught that making profit in this way, taking advantage of your neighbour's needs, was sinful. It had attempted to hedge business activity (except for its own, which it justified as being for the glory of God) around with all sorts of restrictions. But this became increasingly difficult to do as business activity expanded and profit-making became more important. As Church teaching became more and more out of step with the way society was developing, so, in Britain and some other European countries, that Church was itself reformed, in the middle of the 16th century, and, in the process, brought more into line with the ideas and ambitions of the rising merchant classes. This was the beginning of Protestantism.

Of course, there were many factors at work in the movement to re-form the Church. There were those who were disgusted with the Church's own abuses, particularly its selling of the means of salvation for cash; there were those who were greedy to get their hands on the Church's wealth and lands; and there

Peasants had to give money or goods every year to the local priest. This added to their hardship and discontent.

were those rulers (like Henry VIII) who no longer wanted to acknowledge the Pope as their superior. But out of all this mixture of motives and interests came the most important and far-reaching effect of the Reformation, which was to distinguish and finally to separate spiritual matters and spiritual life from business matters and economic life. The Church should still concern itself with the first, but its power and influence over the second was greatly reduced.

The merchant capitalists were then able at last to shed any lingering religious doubts they might have had about the nature of their business, and were quick to finance colonial ventures. For the new colonies would provide the new markets, the new **commodities** and luxury items which the merchants needed to develop and expand their activities.

The colonial trade

The rulers of the colonising countries backed such enterprises with their greater military power, and were ready to crush savagely any resistance from the local peoples. We have already seen what effect the ruthless determination to secure wealth at any cost had on the native American peoples. Not only were the European rulers frequently in debt to the big financiers (the most wealthy and powerful of the merchant capitalists), they also had a vested interest in taxing the huge profits that could be made, so further building up their power at the expense, wherever possible, of their European rivals for the same markets and the same trade.

Thus the 'trade' that was carried on was firmly under the control of the Europeans, its terms were fixed by them, and the articles traded in dictated by European needs.

Though it may have had haphazard beginnings, the gains from the conquest and control of new lands were so enormous, and so rapid, that more and more of these colonial enterprises were planned and carried out. So rapidly, and over so much of the world, did this colonisation-for-profit spread, along with all the different means of keeping control over the colonies and of getting wealth out of them, that we now talk of it as a system, the colonial system.

We can see its beginnings in the colonies of the Americas, and the trading fort areas dotted about the African and Asian coasts, but it was forced at later stages on to all those areas of the world that we now call the Third World, to exploit them for food, **raw materials** and cheap labour. We shall see how this developed later.

We have now looked at why the merchant capitalists were eager to back colonial ventures, and why their governments were ready to support them, but what part did the colonists, or settlers, themselves play in all of this? And what happened to all the riches that were made, and what was done with all the goods traded in? Human beings, in the form of slaves, were the essential 'item' in that trade.

The rich get richer

To understand this, we again need to loook at some of the developments happening in Europe at the time, particularly with regard to agriculture, which was still the basis of all those societies. Already even in medieval Europe, there were regions where whole areas of land were given over to producing one crop, which was not for the use of the local people (as most medieval farm produce was), but was grown in order to be sold for a profit elsewhere. In addition, in medieval Flanders, for example, people were employed and paid regular wages in order to make wool into cloth – not cloth for themselves to wear, but cloth for merchants to sell abroad, for a profit.

In England, we have already mentioned the beginnings of a movement to enclose the land – that is where the lords found it more and more profitable to turn peasants off the land, fence it round and keep sheep on it, for their wool. By the 15th and 16th centuries, however, the raw wool, instead of being sold to merchants overseas, was being worked into cloth in towns and cities in England, by craftsmen who were often no longer independent traders, but were

Where the raw materials were grown (c.1775)

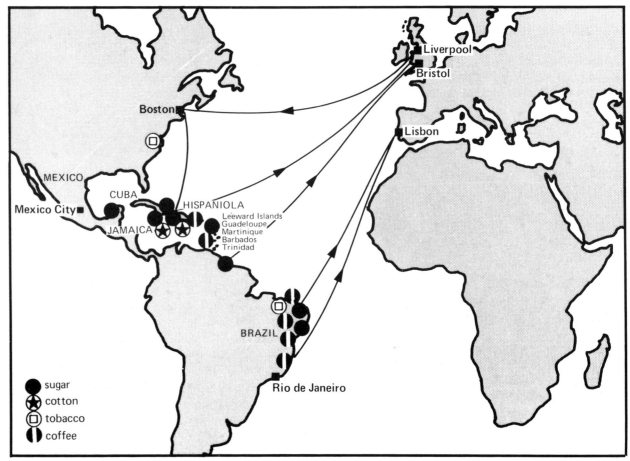

paid wages for their work. The peasants who had been turned off the land – and so could no longer live by growing food for themselves – made their way to the cities, in the hope of finding some work for which they could be paid in money, and so be able to buy their food.

Thus we can see the beginnings of what can be called capitalist enterprises, where people no longer live directly off the land, growing and making what they themselves need, but where a few people own the land, the animals, the tools, the workshops and so on, control what is grown and made, how it is

'The story of a piece of sugar', a 19th century drawing showing the various stages in sugar production.

produced, and what price it is sold at. They use the work of others, who depend on them for wages and therefore their very existence, to make profits which they use as they want.

The early colonists

With the upsurge in colonialism, such a system of organising **production** on a large scale, and for profit, received a tremendous boost. For those early colonists were also looking for the most effective and profitable way to exploit the lush tracts of land they had seized. Firstly, the growing of crops and raw materials in the colonies came to be organised on capitalist lines (using slaves to do all the work) – that is, not for immediate use but for sale. Secondly, the raw materials that were produced on such a large scale were not only essential for the rapid development of European industries, but actually forced European industries to expand, in order to cope with these greater and greater quantities.

White gold

This expansion becomes easier to understand if we look at some historical examples, so let us turn to those early colonies of the West Indies. Since the beginning of the 17th century, the West Indian islands had been

> Many African rulers tried to minimise the damage done by the slave raids and the slave trade. The King of the Kongo (modern Angola), who had welcomed Christian missions into his country, requested doctors, teachers and technical assistance in exchange. He exhorted the Portuguese to end the raids, without success. Tens of thousands of slaves were shipped from Angola.

Olaudah Equiano, who was himself taken as a slave became one of the leading campaigners for its abolition.

increasingly colonised by the British, French and Dutch. Once the islands had been plundered for all they were worth, the next step for the settlers who went there was to make a success of agriculture.

To do this they had to find a crop which could not be grown in Europe – either because of climate, or because of the more pressing need to grow staple food crops there – and for which they could find a market. Obviously, the more intensively such a crop could be grown, the greater the financial reward. Such a crop would be a luxury crop – the appetite of wealthy Europeans for 'luxury' items had already been whetted in the early days of the overland trade. The first crop they tried successfully was tobacco (whose cultivation they learnt from the native peoples

The work involved in sugar production was continuous, back-breaking and unpleasant labour. Here slaves are feeding the furnaces with crushed sugar cane.

Further reading

Lennox Honychurch, *The Caribbean people*. Book 2
    (London, Nelson Caribbean, 1980), Chapters 11 and 12.
Leo Huberman, *Man's Worldly Goods*, part 1.
P. Patterson and J. Carnegie, *The people who came*. Book 2
    (Harlow, Longman Caribbean, 1970), Chapter 16.
R. Unstead, *The medieval scene* (London, A.C. Black, 1962).

Suggestions for work

What foods did people live on in Europe in the 15th and 16th centuries? How do these differ from the foods that are eaten in Britain today? What foods are now grown here that were first introduced from other countries? What do you buy or eat, or see in the supermarket, that can't be grown here and has to be imported?

Find out what the life of a rich merchant would have been like in this period. What sort of household would he have lived in? How would he have carried on his business and what would he have traded in?

What can you find out about sugar growing and the buying and selling of sugar? Where was it grown and how were the plantations organised?

of the Americas). Tobacco had been a great success in Europe when Raleigh brought some back from Virginia.

About the middle of the 17th century, sugar was introduced and was an immediate success – so much so that it became known as 'white gold'. To be most profitable, however, sugar needed to be produced on a large scale; the cane had to be grown on large plantations, and the first stages of its refining had to be carried out on the plantations as well. The quantities involved meant that a factory-type system had to be developed to cope with them. Such operations obviously needed **investment** (to set up the whole system) and a large workforce, the cheaper the better, for which, as we shall see, slaves from Africa were used. The profits to be made from sugar produced along these lines meant that it rapidly ousted the cultivation of other crops. For all these reasons, and because of the scale and swiftness with which sugar cultivation took over enormous areas of the West Indies (and the mainland of Latin America), it marked an extremely significant stage in the development of the capitalist system of producing goods.

CHAPTER FIVE

The colonial system and the Industrial Revolution

But those early colonies were not only important as places where capitalist methods were tried out on a larger scale than ever before. They were important because of the wealth they produced – both through the enormous boost they gave to the worldwide trade controlled by Europe, and for the goods they actually produced for Europe. For the bulk of this wealth flooded back one way or another to Europe. The planters themselves grew immensely rich – and once they had made their pile, they bought great landed estates to live on 'back home' (while their plantations continued to bring in the profits).

In Britain, for example, some of this wealth was used not only to maintain lavish households, but was

Robert Owen's mills and workers' housing in New Lanark.

invested in new enterprises or agricultural experiments. But more than this, raw materials came in month by month from the colonies to be bought, used and sold, in any and every way that could be devised, while the colonies were a guaranteed market for any manufactured goods that Europe could produce.

Without the wealth gained from colonial trade and commerce, and from the capitalist production of sugar in the West Indies in particular, there would not have been the wealth to fuel what we have come to call the Industrial Revolution. This got off the ground in Britain in the middle of the 18th century, and made first Britain, and then other European powers, and North America, even more wealthy and powerful than before.

The Industrial Revolution consisted of the successful, practical application of new

Many grandiose houses were built in England in the 18th and 19th centuries out of the profits from slavery and sugar in the West Indies, or the colonial trade in India. Dodington Park (left) was built in the 18th century by the Codrington family who owned huge plantations in the West Indies. Sezincote (right) was rebuilt by Sir Charles Cockerell in 1805, out of the fortune he made from the East India Company.

developments in science and technology to the production of goods. All these new inventions enabled those who were in the business of making and selling goods to produce them on a much greater scale, at less cost and more efficiently than had previously been possible.

The way in which this production of goods was organised was on capitalist lines, as we described earlier. The men and women who make up the workforce of the factories own nothing, they cannot live by buying and selling like the merchant. They cannot live by growing their own food like the medieval peasant – the land that their grandparents might once have held is now concentrated in the hands of a few. All they have is themselves, all they can sell is their time and their ability to work in exchange for the wage they receive from the manufacturer. By contrast, the manufacturer owns the factory they work in and the machines they work on.

Inside a textile mill. What the picture does not show is that the air would be choking with dust.

He is able to buy the raw materials that they turn into cloth, or pots and pans, or whatever. He sells the finished goods, and pockets the profit. Like the merchant, his aim is to buy cheap and sell dear – the time of his workers and the raw materials cheap, the finished goods dear.

Cotton wealth

Cotton itself – the raw material of the industry which, above all others, spearheaded the Industrial Revolution – was produced on slave plantations in the Americas and the West Indies. The textile industry could never have taken off as it did in Britain if the cotton itself had not been available so cheaply and in virtually unlimited quantities.

The development of other successful industries followed on the heels of the textile industry. The production of James Watt's steam engine was financed directly by profits from the West Indian trade – and think how important that was in industry and trade. Other investments were made in the iron industry (vital in industrial development) and in the railways. Banking and insurance firms which are household names today – Barclays, Lloyds, Williams Deacons – grew directly out of the activities and

Profits from the West Indies helped finance the Great Western Railway.

James Watt, the scientist, is obviously deep in thought here, perhaps even on the verge of his discovery. It was finance from slavery that enabled his idea to become a reality.

profits of the West Indian merchants, the slave holders and the slave traders. For, as trade and industry became more complex, banks and finance houses became increasingly important in ensuring that the system functioned smoothly. They would be on hand to make sure that some potentially profitable enterprise was not nipped in the bud for want of the ready cash to charter the ships or buy the materials and equipment needed. This was, of course, in return for a slice of the profits themselves.

But the West Indies were not the only source of wealth that fed into Britain's development. There had also been a steady influx of wealth from the trade with India, which grew to massive proportions after the East India Company conquered, took over and plundered the rich province of Bengal. It was no coincidence that, only a few years after the decisive battle of Plassey (in 1757), the new inventions and the

A mid-19th century cartoon, showing the relationship of CAPITAL and LABOUR (from Punch*). Notice, however, that labour shown does not include that of black peoples, in the colonies – though this was one of the most essential elements in the whole system.*

19

Factory children scavenging in a pig's trough for food. In Britain, children were the cheapest labour of all – and their small size meant that they could get under and behind machines to clean and tend them.

colonies, and that profit feeding into and making more profitable capitalist methods of organising production in the 'mother countries', a worldwide system for exploiting the labour of men and women, and the natural resources of the world, grew up. Its prime motive was profit. The system was one in which the ruling countries used both their own raw materials and those of their colonies, together with the labour of the European working class and that of the colonies, to mass-produce goods to sell both at home and in the colonies. Once again, the ruling countries got richer, while the colonies got poorer.

Further reading

(* indicates more difficult texts)

* E. Hobsbawm, *The age of revolution: Europe 1789-1848* (London, Weidenfeld and Nicolson, 1962), Chapter 2.
L. Honychurch, *The Caribbean people.* Book 2
Leo Huberman, *Man's worldly goods*, especially Chapters 14 to 16.
* Walter Rodney, *How Europe underdeveloped Africa* (London, Bogle L'Ouverture, 1972).
* E. Williams, *Capitalism and Slavery* (London, Longman, 1964).

Suggestions for work

Where was cotton grown? Why was it so profitable? What new inventions under the Industrial Revolution made cotton cloth so much quicker to produce?

Discuss what happened when it was no longer woven in their cottages by handloom weavers but mass produced in factories.

Discuss how you think slavery and colonialism contributed to Britain's social and economic development.

new technologies of the Industrial Revolution began to be put into effect. For though the idea or principle of an invention may have existed for many years or even centuries (the ancient Greeks had worked out the principle of steam power), there has to be both a need for it in society, and the money put into it, to develop it as a practical piece of equipment.

From these beginnings, then, with capitalist methods proving immensely profitable in the

GINNING COTTON BY STEAM

Production of raw cotton in North America. Here slaves are carrying out the initial process of separating the seed from the fibre. Production was speeded up by the introduction of steam machinery.

CHAPTER SIX

Slavery and racism

The demand for slaves

There is one vital element of this early capitalism and colonial commerce which we have not yet discussed in detail; yet without it, the whole system would have foundered: slave labour. The early colonists in the New World had relied first, on the native American peoples and then, on white 'indentured servants' from Europe to work their tobacco and cotton plantations.

The native Americans, who had been ravaged

A poor man in Europe might be kidnapped and sent to the New World as an indentured servant.

African slaves washing for diamonds in Brazil.

physically and economically by the Spanish and Portuguese conquest, could not endure in addition this harsh and servile labour. They resisted, to death. Their numbers were **decimated** by European diseases against which they had no immunity. Where they had based their way of life on settled agriculture, the whole fabric of their societies, and the fruitfulness of their lands, was destroyed by the European conquest and the establishment of plantations and mines. Whilst some were settled agriculturalists, others lived lives based on hunting animals and gathering wild foods – but all were totally disrupted. Their whole relationship to the land, in and on which they had lived freely, was destroyed so ruthlessly and suddenly that they themselves could scarce survive.

They certainly could not adapt to the new regime of forced labour, either as cultivators of the land or as workers in the mines, that the colonists subjected them to.

The colonists simply saw them as weak and inefficient. A prominent official in Hispaniola insisted in 1518 that 'permission be given to bring in Negroes, a race robust for labour, instead of natives, so weak that they can only be employed in tasks requiring little endurance, such as taking care of maize fields or farms'.

The white labourers were able to stand up to the hard work and harsh treatment – but had the disadvantage (for the planters) that they had to be freed after the term of their contract was over – usually five or ten years. They then expected to receive a plot of land of their own. After a while, it became impossible to maintain a sufficient supply of white indentured labour, and when sugar was introduced into the West Indies, the land available for the smallholdings of the poor whites got swallowed up by the large plantations that were necessary to make sugar profitable.

For the profit-hungry planters there was only one solution: slave labour from Africa. The slave was cheaper; money which might buy a white man's services for ten years, would buy a slave for life.

The slave trade

From the middle of the 17th century, the trade in black slaves from Africa – to work the tobacco and then the cotton plantations of North America, the mines, coffee, cocoa and sugar plantations of Latin America, and the sugar plantations of the West Indies – grew until it reached massive proportions, both in terms of profit and of people.

What this meant for Africa was terrible disruption to its societies, because of the enormous and continuing loss of its young, able-bodied men and women. At the time when Europeans first made inroads into Africa,

RADIO TIMES HULTON

Songhay was one of the ancient empires of Western Africa, whose principal city, Timbuctu, was a centre of trade and learning. A detailed account of it was published in Italy in 1550 and caused a great sensation.

66 There you find many judges, professors and devout men all handsomely maintained by the king who holds scholars in much honour. There too, they sell many handwritten North African books and more profit is made there from the sale of books than from any other branch of trade. **99**

there were many different forms of society within the continent – with flourishing trade networks, the development in different regions of clothworking, gold mining, iron making, different forms of agriculture, fine cities, great temples and churches and monuments, skilfully made works of art. But much of this development was slowly bled to death, making the continent ultimately defenceless against the full colonial conquest that was to follow – for it was not until towards the end of the 19th century that Europe was powerful enough to subdue Africa completely.

What the slave trade meant for Europe was an enormous injection of profit and wealth that enabled its own industrial development to flourish, together with, as we shall see, a legacy of racism that is still embedded in European culture.

In terms of profit, slaves were valuable in two ways: as commodities to be traded in, and as producers of crops and raw materials. They were the essential element in what came to be known as the 'triangular trade'. It is easiest to understand how this worked if you study the map. This trade was immensely profitable. At each stage of the journey there was a transaction – and profit – to be made.

Having made a profit for their buyers and sellers, the slaves were then set to work on the plantations to produce the sugar, cotton and tobacco that the colonists sold to the home or 'mother' country. Since the slaves were only given the bare minimum on which to live, and since they were worked till they dropped, their labour was the cheapest possible – thus enabling the plantation owner to make the greatest possible profit.

The growth of racism

Although, as we have seen, African people were taken and used by Europeans as slaves in the New World for economic reasons, there was an element of **racialism** in this choice. It can be seen if we simply ask ourselves the question: why were Europeans taken on

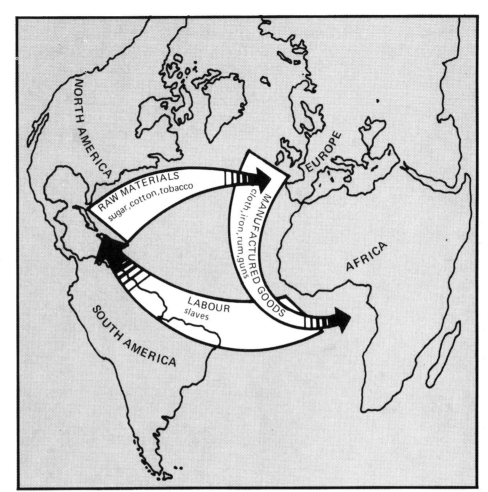

The 'triangular trade'

Ships sailed from the 'mother country' with manufactured goods, which they exchanged on the West Coast of Africa for slaves.

The cargoes of slaves were taken across the Atlantic (the journey became known as the 'Middle Passage') and sold in the West Indies, North and South America, to work on the plantations there.

The same ships were then loaded with the products of the plantations, i.e. food, luxuries and raw materials, which were taken back and sold in the 'mother country'.

Thus, the slave trade, or the 'triangular trade' as it became known, made profits at each of its three stages – profits which went to the merchant capitalists who financed it, and which made seaport towns like Bristol and Liverpool very wealthy indeed.

as indentured servants, and Africans as slaves? Or, to put it another way, why was it considered acceptable to turn African people into property, but not fellow Europeans?

We must remember that slavery had existed since the earliest times – slaves were often captives from war. There was a flourishing slave trade in the early Middle Ages around the Mediterranean, as well as a trade in African slaves carried on by Arab merchants. In the 12th century, the Italians were using slaves,

people who had been captured in war and then bought and sold on the slave markets, to grow sugar on the island of Cyprus, which had been taken from the Muslims in the Crusades. Christian merchants in Genoa sold Christian slaves to Muslim Saracens.

The early Christian Church itself owned many slaves, and never seriously contemplated that such an institution should be abolished. But, although in that early period there was no particular objection to the use of Christians as slaves, and the majority of the slaves then were of European origin, by the 15th century, the Church had come round firmly to the view that Christians should not be turned into slaves, if there was an alternative.

But although slavery had existed for centuries, there is a very important distinction to be made between the slavery of the earlier periods, and the enslavement of non-European peoples that was practised under slavery and colonialism. In the earlier periods, by and large slaves were seen and treated as a class within society, a necessary part of the social order, although the very lowest part of it. There were laws and customs to regulate slavery.

Under ancient slavery slaves could obtain their freedom, and even rise to the very top of society. But with colonial slavery, a slave ceased to be regarded as a person at all. A slave had no legal rights or standing, was outside of society altogether, to be regarded and treated solely as a thing, to be bought and sold for profit, and to be used, in the same way that a factory owner would use a machine, to produce whatever was required.

Nevertheless, the fact could not be got round that black people – even black slaves – were human beings, not things. So to justify such a system of treating other human beings, Europeans came to

argue that the Africans they captured, and bought and sold, were not fully human at all. And the basis for such a belief was already there in European culture itself.

Christian teaching and practice

For centuries, Catholicism had held that a person could only be fully human if he or she was a believer within the one true Church. Non-believers, which included of course all those non-European peoples who worshipped different gods under different religious systems, were therefore an inferior sort of human being.

In Europe's early history, this belief had vented itself on the Jews, who – held to be responsible, for

Above: A scene from the Cuban film 'The last supper', depicting a slave revolt on a sugar plantation. Most Europeans, however, preferred to think that slavery was abolished, not because slave rebellions rendered slavery uneconomic, but because of the enlightened efforts of the anti-slavery campaign. This plaque (right), showing a humble slave on his knees, raising his eyes gratefully to heaven, illustrates the abolitionists' way of thinking.

TO BE SOLD, on board the Ship *Bance-Yland*, on tuefday the 6th of *May* next, at *Afhley-Ferry* ; a choice cargo of about 250 fine healthy

NEGROES,

juft arrived from the Windward & Rice Coaft. —The utmoft care has already been taken, and fhall be continued, to keep them free from the leaft danger of being infected with the SMALL-POX, no boat having been on board, and all other communication with people from *Charles-Town* prevented.

Auftin, Laurens, & Appleby.

N. B. Full one Half of the above Negroes have had the SMALL-POX in their own Country. .

A bill of sale for slaves, who were bought and sold like any other commodity.

ever and ever, for the killing of Christ – were subjected to all sorts of tyranny and abuse, as well as being made to do much of the dirty work of business and finance that was considered dangerous for the Christian soul. Attacks on them were frequent – in 1190, 150 Jews were massacred after being besieged in York Castle. At the end of the 13th century Edward I drove the Jews out of England. They were also expelled from France, in the 14th century, and from Spain, in the 15th (in 1492).

There was, therefore, already a basis within European culture for **discriminating** against and abusing a whole people on the grounds of their origin. The assumption was built into European culture that Europeans were somehow superior – an assumption which the dog-eat-dog competition in greed and aggression that had gone on for centuries between European powers had done nothing to dispel.

With the coming of the slave trade, and the institution of slavery on a scale such as the world had never seen before, these elements of European culture took on a new and terrible lease of life. And the very speed and intensity with which the enslavement of Africans was carried out further reinforced the notion that they were not individuals but things.

How they justified slavery

Europeans based their theories of African inferiority on the easily seen physical differences between themselves and the Africans. Thus they began to **rationalise** and justify their treatment of them. In other words, arguments were put forward that, although black people were human beings, they were in all respects inferior human beings.

They were, it was claimed, uncivilised and barbaric (though, at an earlier period, Portuguese

For a long time, Bristol was the premier slave-trading port, and that trade gave a boost to every aspect of its development. This picture, made in 1830, shows the bustle and activity round its by now large and modern harbour.

explorers themselves had been awed by the magnificence of the great African civilisations). They were stupid, but strong (so, of course, only really suited to the arduous, menial tasks of slavery). They were lazy and cunning (if you think this contradicts the earlier statement, then you are right – but logic does not enter into these types of beliefs), and so needed constant and harsh supervision. The colour of their skins was black – associated for centuries in the European mind with darkness, fear, evil and the very opposite and enemy of Christian whiteness and light. And their colour, which was unchangeable, was the visible proof that they themselves could never change, develop or act as anything but slaves and servants to their white masters.

There is a passage in the Bible about the descendants of Noah's son, Ham (who was cursed by God), who are condemned for all eternity to be slaves and servants. In the Middle Ages, this was held by the clergy to apply to the lowest ranks of society, the poorest peasants and the serfs, whose position was considered fixed and unalterable. With the establishment of slavery in the colonial period, it came to be understood to refer exclusively to black people.

Theories of racial superiority

From such crude beginnings, a whole theory of the racial superiority of white people over black was developed, initially to justify the slave system, and eventually to justify all the ways in which non-white people were exploited by the white colonial powers. For though slavery and the slave system came to be abolished (the constant rebellions of the slaves, combined with other economic developments made slavery unprofitable), other ways were found to use the lands, the raw materials and the labour of non-white people to produce high profits for the colonial powers. Hand in hand with these developments, over the years a whole body of 'scientific' arguments was developed and used to justify the actions of the colonial powers.

If people are held to be naturally and forever inferior, then you are justified in ruling them for their own good (and your enormous profit). You are justified in not paying them what their work is worth (so getting cheap labour which adds to your profit), or not paying them the true value of what they do produce. If you study the history of any of the colonies ruled by the European powers, you will see how racist theories and racist practices have been used to create wealth and profit for the colonial masters.

So we can say that **racism** is not just a set of ideas or beliefs, it has a very important economic function. It not only degrades and humiliates, but it also robs and impoverishes, in every way, the peoples who are its target. Racism made the cheap labour force that the capitalist system demanded almost free. The colonies

Bristol again. A sugar refinery in the late 19th century.

MANSELL COLLECTION

were plundered – using that labour force – of the raw materials and natural resources needed to supply the industries of Europe. Europe was enriched and its own development stimulated at terrible cost to the colonial peoples.

So we can see that the colonial and capitalist systems, which grew up together, as we have described in earlier chapters, were also inescapably and inherently racist.

Leonard Parkinson, one of the fighting maroons of Jamaica in the 18th century.

A white plantation owner in the mid-19th century in the West Indies. The men supporting him look on with contempt.

Further reading

(* indicates more difficult texts)

B. Davidson, *Discovering Africa's past* (Harlow, Longman, 1978).

Paul Edwards (ed.), *Equiano's travels* (London, Heinemann, 1970, African Writers Series).

* Philip Foner, *History of Black Americans*, Chapters 4, 5, and 19.

Alex Haley, *Roots* (London, Hutchinson, 1977).

L. Honychurch, *The Caribbean people*, Book 2, Chapter 13.

David Killingray, *The slave trade* (London, Harrap, 1974, World History series).

Milton McFarland, *Cudjoe the Maroon* (London, Allison and Busby, 1977).

Lucille Mathurin, *The rebel women in the British West Indies during slavery* (African Caribbean Publications, for Africa Caribbean Institute of Jamaica, 1975, available in London).

Suggestions for further work

What can you find out about the colonial trade in slaves? Who controlled it and why was it so profitable? How did the slaves resist? Where were they taken and for what purposes?

What can you find out about the slave trade in Europe in the Middle Ages? Discuss how it differed from slavery under colonialism.

It has been estimated that 9-10 million people were taken from Africa as slaves. What effects do you think this had on the societies of Africa? Using Basil Davidson's book for your basic information, write an account of one small group or village whose young people were captured and taken away.

Glossary

Arabic: We call our numbers Arabic because we copied the way to write them from Arabic script.

Astrology: To study the positions of the moon, the sun and other planets, in the belief that these influence the course of human life and so can help in the prediction of the future.

Capitalism: An economic system characterised by the private ownership of the means of production. These owners are called **capitalists** and their main aim is to produce goods to sell at a profit. During the early phase of industrialisation, the major capitalist is the factory owner. However, we can also distinguish the **merchant capitalist** who deals specifically in the buying and selling of wholesale commodities on an international basis (*see also* **MEANS OF PRODUCTION**).

Colonies, colonialism: A process which describes the way in which people from major trading nations settled in other countries to ensure that the 'mother country' was supplied with raw materials. These **colonies** also provided a market for the finished products produced in the 'mother country'.

Commodities: Any goods which satisfy human needs, but generally associated with agricultural products and raw materials which can be traded.

Conquistadores: Generally this means 'conqueror', i.e. someone who takes possession by force. But it is used more specifically in reference to the Spanish conquerors of Mexico and Peru in the 16th century.

Decimate: To destroy or wipe out on a very large scale.

Discriminate against: To treat one particular group of people (marked out by their origin or skin colour) less favourably than others, and unequally with other groups in society – perhaps through laws or social policies which only apply to them.

Expansion: The growth of political and economic influence of one country over other countries.

Exploitation: In this book the term has two broad meanings:
(a) the exploitation of man – occurs when the labour power of the *majority* of the people is used for the benefit of a *minority* of people.
(b) the exploitation of raw materials – in essence, measures which increase the amount of raw materials which are then used for the production of goods.

Indentured: When a contract is signed that binds one person to work for another for a set period, under set terms. Indentured labour contracts are often very unequal in their conditions – the terms they laid down very frequently added up almost to slavery.

Investment: The purchase of machinery and other means of production in order to equip factories so that goods can be produced on a large scale.

Means of production: All the basic requirements for producing goods. They include raw materials, machinery and labour. Taken together these means of production amount to a country's total economic resources.

Nautical: The art of navigation. For instance, a nautical almanac is a record of astronomical and tidal information. Collecting this information makes navigation easier for the sailor.

Navigation: The method whereby the position of the ship can be located and the course that the ship will take can be plotted.

Production: The process by which the means of production (land, labour, capital) are combined together to satisfy human needs.

Profit: The reward of the capitalist, i.e. the owner of the means of production. Usually referred to as a residue – the amount of money left over after all the means of production have been paid for.

Racialism, racism: Throughout these two books we distinguish between racialism and racism. Racialism refers to prejudiced beliefs and behaviour. When, however, these become fully systematised into a philosophy of 'race' superiority, and when this then becomes a part of the way in which society as a whole is organised, then we use the term racism. An individual who acts in a racially prejudiced way is a **racialist**; a society whose most powerful economic and social institutions – industry, law, media, government – are organised on, or in effect act on, the principle that one 'race' is superior to another is **racist**.

Rationalise: In this context it means to explain away – to find justifications for acts or beliefs that are otherwise unjustifiable and to hide real and deeper motives.

Raw materials: One of the major means of production from which goods are produced. Examples of raw materials include rubber, iron ore, cotton, coal, etc.

Surplus: The exchange of goods is known as **trade** and this takes place both within a country, from region to region, and between countries, in the form of imports and exports. In order for trade to take place, a **surplus** must be produced – in other words, that amount of goods which is not required by the producer or the peasantry. This surplus can be sold or traded for other goods. As an economy progresses – in other words, produces more goods – so this surplus increases.